Jennifer Lawrence

Gillian Gosman

PowerKiDS press

New York

Published in 2012 by The Rosen Publishing Group, Inc.
29 East 21st Street, New York, NY 10010

Copyright © 2012 by The Rosen Publishing Group, Inc.

All rights reserved. No part of this book may be reproduced in any form without permission in writing from the publisher, except by a reviewer.

First Edition

Editor: Jennifer Way
Book Design: Kate Laczynski
Layout Design: Julio Gil

Photo Credits: Cover Jon Kopaloff/FilmMagic/Getty Images; p. 4 Jason Merritt/Getty Images; p. 7 Fred Hayes/Getty Images; p. 8 John Shearer/WireImage/Getty Images; p. 11 Eric Charbonneau/WireImage/Getty Images; p. 12 Jesse Grant/WireImage/Getty Images; p. 15 John Shearer/Getty Images for PSFF; p. 16 Dan MacMedan/WireImage/Getty Images; p. 19 Marcel Thomas/FilmMagic/Getty Images; p. 20 Frazer Harrison/Getty Images for AFI.

Library of Congress Cataloging-in-Publication Data

Gosman, Gillian.
 Jennifer Lawrence / by Gillian Gosman. — 1st ed.
   p. cm. — (Kid stars!)
 Includes index.
 ISBN 978-1-4488-6194-1 (library binding) — ISBN 978-1-4488-6349-5 (pbk.) — ISBN 978-1-4488-6350-1 (6-pack)
 1. Lawrence, Jennifer, 1990-—Juvenile literature. 2. Actors—United States—Biography—Juvenile literature. I. Title.
 PN2287.L28948G58 2012
 791.4302'8092—dc23
 [B]
2011030841

Manufactured in the United States of America

CPSIA Compliance Information: Batch #WW12PK: For Further Information contact Rosen Publishing, New York, New York at 1-800-237-9932

Contents

Meet Jennifer Lawrence 5
Jennifer's Childhood 6
Getting Started 9
Ready for Prime Time 10
On the Big Screen 13
Winter's Bone 14
And the Winner Is 17
Hunger Games 18
Lawrence Offscreen 21
Fun Facts 22
Glossary 23
Index 24
Web Sites 24

Jennifer has said that she really enjoys acting in small, serious movies. She says that she has to use her imagination to play some of these parts because the dark roles are nothing like her life!

Meet Jennifer Lawrence

There are many young actresses trying to make it big in Hollywood, but Jennifer Lawrence stands out. She has played roles in television comedies. She is an **athlete** who shines in action-adventure movies. She takes on serious, difficult roles in small movies. It seems she can do it all.

Although she has had no training as an actress, Jennifer is a favorite among fans and **critics**. It looks like she is just at the beginning of a long, exciting **career** in movies!

Jennifer's Childhood

Jennifer Shrader Lawrence was born in Louisville, Kentucky, on August 15, 1990. She grew up on a farm in Kentucky with her parents, Gary and Karen, and her two older brothers, Ben and Blaine.

As a young girl, Jennifer was very athletic. She was a cheerleader and she also played field hockey and softball. Jennifer also **modeled**. She acted in plays at her church, but it took a while before she realized acting was her passion. When she decided she wanted to be an actress, she asked her parents to help her follow this dream.

From left to right are Jennifer, Jennifer's mother, Jennifer's publicist Liz Mahoney, and actress Casey MacLaren. They are at the 2010 Sundance Film Festival, in Park City, Utah.

Once a movie is done, actors often answer questions after a screening of the movie. Here, Lawrence is answering questions after a 2011 screening of the movie *Winter's Bone*.

Getting Started

In spring 2004, Jennifer traveled to New York City. She was just 14 years old. She **auditioned** for **agents** by performing cold readings of scripts. At a cold reading, an actor reads **dialogue** out loud for the first time in front of agents. Cold readings are difficult to do, but Jennifer's auditions were a big success.

The agents asked Jennifer to spend the summer in New York City, and she agreed. That summer, she appeared in commercials. Acting in commercials is often how an actor gets started in show business.

Ready for Prime Time

Soon after Jennifer spent the summer in New York, her family decided to move to Los Angeles, California, so that Jennifer could spend more time on her acting career. Jennifer also finished high school in 2006, two years early, so that she could focus on her career. These decisions paid off. Between 2006 and 2007, she appeared on **episodes** of the **prime-time** television shows *Medium*, *Monk*, and *Cold Case*.

In 2007, Jennifer won the role of Lauren Pearson on the TBS sitcom *The Bill Engvall Show*. The show was about the Pearson family, led by father Bill, a doctor, and his wife, Susan. Jennifer played Bill and Susan's oldest child, Lauren.

Here is Jennifer (right) in 2007 with Bill Engvall (left) and Skyler Gisondo (second from left) of *The Bill Engvall Show* and TBS vice president Michael Wright (center).

11

Lawrence (left) costarred with Charlize Theron (right) in *The Burning Plain*. They are shown here at the 2008 Venice Film Festival, in Italy, where Lawrence won the Marcello Mastroianni Award for Best Young Actress.

On the Big Screen

The Bill Engvall Show was on television for three seasons, from 2007 until 2009. After that show ended, Lawrence earned roles in several small movies, *Garden Party*, *The Poker House*, *The Burning Plain*, and *Devil You Know*. In these four movies, Lawrence had the chance to work with some of Hollywood's big stars, including Charlize Theron, Kim Basinger, and Selma Blair.

Lawrence's performances in these movies earned awards and praise from critics. She won an award at the 2008 Los Angeles Film Festival for her acting in *The Poker House*. This helped her get noticed for bigger, starring roles.

Winter's Bone

In 2009, Lawrence was cast as the star of *Winter's Bone*, a movie based on a 2006 novel of the same name by Daniel Woodrell. The movie tells the story of Ree Dolly, a poor teenage girl living in the country and taking care of her sick mother and her younger sister and brother. Their life is hard, especially when it looks like they might lose their house. Ree faces threatening criminals and risks her life in her quest to save her family's house.

Critics loved *Winter's Bone*, and they praised Lawrence's acting. It was her **breakthrough** performance. She had become a star!

Lawrence got lots of praise for her role in *Winter's Bone*. Here, she is accepting the Rising Star Award during the 2011 Palm Springs International Film Festival, in California.

Here is Lawrence on the red carpet before the Academy Awards in 2011. She was nominated for Best Actress for playing Ree Dolly in *Winter's Bone*. Natalie Portman ended up winning the award that year.

And the Winner Is . . .

Lawrence won an award at the Los Angeles Film Festival for her role in *The Poker House*. She also won an award at the Venice Film Festival for her work in *The Burning Plain*.

Winter's Bone, though, brought Lawrence lots of **nominations** and awards. The movie won the Grand Jury Prize for dramas at the Sundance Film Festival, and Lawrence won an award from the Seattle International Film Festival for her part in the movie. Maybe most exciting, though, was Lawrence's nomination for an Academy Award for Best Actress for *Winter's Bone*. That is one of the biggest honors an actor can receive.

Hunger Games

In 2011, movie fans were excited to learn that Lawrence had been cast as Katniss Everdeen in *The Hunger Games*, a movie based on Suzanne Collins's popular young-adult novel of the same name.

People loved the book and the character of Katniss so much that the filmmakers knew they would have a hard time finding just the right person to play this tough, smart character in the movie. They auditioned about 30 different actresses before deciding that Lawrence was the perfect choice to play Katniss. She had to do a lot of physical training to play this part, and her natural athletic ability helped her with this preparation.

Lawrence had to change her hair color to brown to play Katniss in *The Hunger Games*. Here she is after a 2011 appearance on the *Late Show with David Letterman*.

Lawrence has become good friends with Lauren Sweetser, with whom she costarred in *Winter's Bone*. Here the friends are showing off plaques from the American Film Institute honoring *Winter's Bone*.

Lawrence Offscreen

Lawrence's acting career has taken off, and she always seems to be working on a new movie. After *Winter's Bone*, she appeared in *The Beaver*, *Like Crazy*, *House at the End of the Street*, and *X-Men: First Class*.

Lawrence still makes time for her friends and family, though. Even a rising Hollywood star like Lawrence needs time with the people closest to her. Lawrence also works to help others between acting jobs. She has been an assistant to nurses on a church trip to the Dominican Republic as well as at a summer camp.

FUN FACTS

 Lawrence auditioned for the role of Bella Swan in *Twilight*. The role went to Kristen Stewart, though.

 Jennifer's childhood nickname was Nitro.

 Today, the Lawrence family runs a summer day camp on the farmland where Jennifer grew up.

 Lawrence appeared in the music video for the song "The Mess I Made" by the band Parachute.

 Jennifer's first paying acting job was in an advertisement for MTV's *My Super Sweet Sixteen*.

 Unlike most young stars, Lawrence does not have an account on Facebook or Twitter.

 Jennifer finished her high-school degree by taking online classes. She had a 3.9 grade point average.

 To play the part of Mystique in *X-Men: First Class*, Lawrence had to sit in a chair for 8 hours every day getting her makeup done!

 It took 3 hours to take off her Mystique makeup!

 Lawrence lives in Santa Monica, California.

Glossary

agents (AY-jents) People who help writers, actors, or sports players with their jobs.

athlete (ATH-leet) Someone who takes part in sports.

auditioned (ah-DIH-shund) Tried out.

breakthrough (BRAYK-throo) Having to do with a person's first big success.

career (kuh-REER) A job.

critics (KRIH-tiks) People who write their opinions about things.

dialogue (DY-uh-lawg) Part of a written work with two or more characters speaking.

episodes (EH-puh-sohdz) Parts of a TV series that are shown at the same time each week.

modeled (MAH-duld) Appeared wearing, using, or posing with a product.

nominations (nah-muh-NAY-shunz) Suggestions that people or things should be given awards or positions.

prime-time (PRYM-tym) Having to do with the time during which most people watch television.

Index

A
agents, 9
athlete, 5

B
Bill Engvall Show, The, 10, 13

C
church, 6
critics, 5, 13–14

F
fans, 5, 18

H
high school, 10
Hunger Games, The, 18

L
Louisville, Kentucky, 6

S
Sundance Film Festival, 17

W
Winter's Bone, 14, 17, 21

X
X-Men: First Class, 21–22

Web Sites

Due to the changing nature of Internet links, PowerKids Press has developed an online list of Web sites related to the subject of this book. This site is updated regularly. Please use this link to access the list:
www.powerkidslinks.com/kids/law/